HOW LONG IS NEVER?

DARFUR – A RESPONSE

HOW LONG IS NEVER?

DARFUR – A RESPONSE

Michael Bhim
Amy Evans
Jennifer Farmer
Carlo Gébler
Juliet Alicia Gilkes
Lynn Nottage
Winsome Pinnock

JOSEF WEINBERGER PLAYS

LONDON

HOW LONG IS NEVER? DARFUR – A RESPONSE
First published in 2007
by Josef Weinberger Ltd
12-14 Mortimer Street, London, W1T 3JJ
www.josef-weinberger.com   general.info@jwmail.co.uk

Copyright © 2007 by Michael Bhim, Amy Evans, Jennifer Farmer, Carlo Gébler, Juliet Alicia Gilkes, Lynn Nottage and Winsome Pinnock.

The authors assert their moral right to be identified as the authors of the works.

ISBN 978 0 85676 299 4

The plays in this volume are protected by Copyright. According to Copyright Law, no public performance or reading of a protected play or part of that play may be given without prior authorisation from Josef Weinberger Plays, as agent for the Copyright Owners.

From time to time it is necessary to restrict or even withdraw the rights of certain plays. **It is therefore essential to check with us before making a commitment to produce a play.**

NO PERFORMANCE MAY BE GIVEN WITHOUT A LICENCE

AMATEUR PRODUCTIONS
Royalties are due at least one calendar month prior to the first performance. A royalty quotation will be issued upon receipt of the following details:

Name of Licensee
Place of Performance
Dates and Number of Performances
Audience Capacity
Ticket Prices

PROFESSIONAL PRODUCTIONS
All enquiries regarding professional rights (other than first class rights) should be addressed to Josef Weinberger at the address above. Enquiries for all other rights should be addressed to the author's agents:
Michael Bhim – David Higham Associates, 5-8 Lower John Street, Golden Square, London W1F 9HA.
Amy Evans – The Agency (London) Ltd, 24 Pottery Lane, Holland Park, London W11 4LZ.
Jennifer Farmer – Micheline Steinberg Associates Ltd, 104 Great Portland Street, London W1W 6PE. info@steinplays.com
Carlo Gébler – Antony Harwood Ltd, 103 Walton Street, Oxford OX2 6EB.
Juliet Alicia Gilkes – Micheline Steinberg Associates Ltd, 104 Great Portland Street, London W1W 6PE. info@steinplays.com
Lynn Nottage – The Gersh Agency, 41 Madison Avenue, 33rd Floor, New York, NY 10010 USA.
Winsome Pinnock – Casarotto Ramsay & Associates Ltd, Waverley House, 7-12 Noel Street, London W1F 8GQ.

OVERSEAS PRODUCTIONS

Applications for productions overseas should be addressed to our local authorised agents. Further details are listed in our catalogue of plays, published every two years, or available from Josef Weinberger Plays at the address above.

CONDITIONS OF SALE

This book is sold subject to the condition that it shall not by way of trade or otherwise be resold, hired out, circulated or distributed without prior consent of the Publisher. **Reproduction of the text either in whole or part and by any means is strictly forbidden.**

SPECIAL NOTE

The authors and the publisher will be donating a percentage of all income received from the sale of this book and from performance royalties of the plays contained herein to the Aegis Trust, an independent, international organisation dedicated to eliminating genocide in Darfur. For more information visit: www.aegistrust.org

Printed by Commercial Colour Press plc, Hainault, Essex

ABOUT THE AUTHORS

Michael Bhim – Distant Violence
Michael graduated from the Royal Court Theatre Advanced Playwrights course in July 2004 and since then has had his short play *Night Moves* performed at the Pleasance Theatre, and various readings of work in progress at the Soho Theatre and the Royal Court Theatre. In November 2005 he won the Alfred Fagon Award for the play *Daydreams of Haily*, and in May 2006 was selected to take part in a year-long attachment with Paines Plough Theatre Company called Future Perfect. His play *Pure Gold* is under option to Soho Theatre, where he is currently working under the Writer Attachment Programme. *Distant Violence* has been nominated for the 2007 Meyer Whitworth Award.

Amy Evans – Many Men's Wife
Amy was born in North Carolina and lived in Germany for several years before moving to London, where she completed an MA in Performance Writing at Goldsmith's College. She has taught and lead workshops at Humboldt University in Berlin and Fordham University in New York, and has been a member of the Tricycle Writer's Group for several years. Her first play, *Achidi J's Final Hours*, was joint winner of the Verity Bargate Award in 2002 and premiered the following year at the Finborough Theatre. More recently, her play *UnStoned* premiered at the Soho Theatre in 2006 as part of the National Youth Theatre's fiftieth anniversary festival *Sextet*.

Jennifer Farmer – words, words, words
Jennifer was born in Chattanooga, Tennessee. She received a BFA (honours) in Dramatic Writing from New York University, Tisch School of the Arts prior to moving to London. *Bulletproof Soul* was produced at Birmingham Rep in the spring of 2007, and her play *Compact Failure* received rave reviews during its national tour in 2004. She has also written *And the Guns are Getting Louder* for the Red Room, *Times Being What They Are* for the Bush Theatre as the 2004/5 Sheila Lemon Writer in Residence and a short monologue as part of *I Confess* at Hoxton Hall during 2006.

Carlo Gébler – Silhouette
Carlo was born in Dublin, brought up in London and now lives outside Enniskillen in Northern Ireland. He is the author of

novels, including *The Eleventh Summer*, *The Cure* and *How to Murder a Man* as well as fiction for children, short stories and works of non-fiction including *The Siege of Derry: A History* and the memoir *Father & I*. He is currently writer-in-residence at HMP Maghaberry. His adaptation of August Strindberg's *Dance of Death* and his play *10 Rounds* have both been produced at the Tricycle Theatre, London.

Juliet Alicia Gilkes – Bilad al-Sudan
Juliet Alicia lives in London where she works as a playwright and television journalist. She has reported in countries including Ethiopia, Haiti and the Dominican Republic. In Cuba she explored the African Diaspora after winning the BBC's Alexander Onassis Bursary. Her plays include *At the Gates of Gaza, Brethren, Good Iago* (Nottingham Playhouse), and *Diesel,* following an attachment to the NT Studio.

Lynn Nottage – Give, Again?
Lynn is from Brooklyn. Her play *Intimate Apparel* was recently premiered at Center Stage and South Coast Rep. Her other plays include *A Walk Through Time* (a children's musical), *Crumbs from the Table of Joy, Mud River Stone, Por'knockers, Poof!, Las Meninas* and *Fabulation, or the Re-Education of Undine*, all of which have been extensively produced Off-Broadway and regionally in the USA. *Fabulation* was first produced in the UK at the Tricycle Theatre, where it received two very successful runs during 2006. She is a member of New Dramatists, a graduate of Brown University and the Yale School of Drama, where she is currently a visiting lecturer in playwriting.

Winsome Pinnock – IDP
Winsome is a graduate of Goldsmith's College and Birkbeck College (both University of London). Her plays for the stage include *One Under* (Tricycle), *Stowaway* (Theatre Royal, Plymouth), *The Wind of Change* (Half Moon Theatre) *Leave Taking* (Liverpool Playhouse Studio; Royal National Theatre; Lyric Studio Hammersmith), *Picture Palace* (Women's Theatre Group), *A Hero's Welcome* (Women's Playhouse Trust at the Royal Court Theatre Upstairs), *Talking in Tongues* (Royal Court Theatre Upstairs), *Mules* (Clean Break at the Royal Court Theatre Upstairs; Mark Taper Forum, Los Angeles; Magic Theatre, San Francisco), and *Water* (Tricycle). Work for television includes the screenplays *Bitter Harvest, Chalk Face* and *South of the Border* (all BBC). Winsome is currently part time lecturer in Creative Writing at London Metropolitan University.

FOREWORD

Since the beginning of the new Millennium, Darfur had been haunting the news bulletins. The death toll seemed to be endlessly rising, the food crisis getting worse and the peace talks moving from stalled to breakdown. To most Westerners, the situation was even more confused, because of the North/South civil war in the Sudan which overlapped with the crisis in the Darfur region. Added to that, the invasion of Iraq by the West had made even humanitarian intervention in other Muslim nations' internal affairs more difficult. The debate over whether this was genocide, whether the African Union Forces could cope without full UN intervention and whether the Sudanese government had either the will or the wish to resolve the situation continued and continues unabated.

One Saturday May morning last year, I heard Mia Farrow talking on the *Today Programme* on Radio 4. She had just come back from Darfur which she had visited as a UNICEF representative. She was talking eloquently about the situation there, and when asked by the interviewer what people could do as the situation seemed so hopeless, she responded by saying that, "we all have a duty to do something to ensure that this crisis did not slip off the international agenda". I had long been troubled by my ignorance about Darfur and this interview was both moving and a spur to action.

Five years ago, the Tricycle had set up a writers' group (sponsored by Bloomberg) in order to support black and Asian theatre writers. This was a loosely-knit group equally divided between male and female writers, and those with much stage experience and some relative newcomers. The group met about five or six times a year for discussions or workshops, and we had arranged a writers' weekend workshop for that same Saturday as the *Today Programme* broadcast.

During the morning of the workshop, whilst the writers were working on their scripts, I downloaded a recording of the interview from the internet and in the lunch break I played it to all the writers. They were very moved by Mia Farrow's words, and when I suggested that we took up her challenge and wrote something in response to the situation in Darfur, there was an immediate enthusiasm for the project.

After some discussion it was agreed that the writers who were interested in taking part should be set a deadline of the end of August 2006 to submit a ten to twenty minute script. The brief was that it could be any response the writer had to the situation in the Sudan, but it must be cast from amongst the actors who were playing in our current production of Lynn Nottage's *Fabulation*.

Included into this challenge were two other writers: Lynn Nottage, whose play *Fabulation* was the last play in our African-American season in 2006, and Carlo Gébler, who two years previously, I had commissioned to write a play about Darfur. Carlo generously agreed to make available to us his written research on the subject.

What came out of this exercise was a predominantly black, and a predominantly female response to Darfur. It was a very enlightening process for all of us, and I hope it will be similarly so for everyone who reads, performs or sees these plays.

Nicolas Kent
February 2007

BACKGROUND TO THE CRISIS IN DARFUR

Darfur is a region the size of France in Western Sudan. Just over half of the six million people who live in Darfur are black Africans; the rest are Arab. The present situation has polarised tribal groups, but in previous generations, ethnic identity was more fluid as groups were Islamised and Arabised. Despite severe underdevelopment in the region, the tribal groups have a long history of co-existence. They intermarried and often one group was indistinguishable from another.

In the 1980s drought worsened the situation in the already underdeveloped region. Rather than address the problem, the Sudanese Government questioned the right of Africans to live in Darfur. In recent years Africans have increasingly been referred to as *abid* meaning 'slave' and *zurga*, a term equivalent to 'nigger'. They have been viewed as inferior to the Arab population.

Between 2003 and 2007 Africans have been killed and driven from the region. This is a large-scale military operation targeting the men, women and children of the African population in Darfur. The Government of Sudan has armed Arab militia (Janjaweed) who have terrorized and burned African villages with the support of the Sudanese army and airforce.

In February 2005 the UK Foreign Office stated that the death toll could be as high as 400,000.[1] More than 3,000 African villages have been burned.[2] Rape is rife and aerial bombardment has been a common occurrence. Conditions of life impossible for human survival have been imposed. Two million people have been displaced. These internally displaced people (IDPs) are unable to leave the IDP camps for fear of Janjaweed attack. They rely upon humanitarian aid.

Not all Darfur Arabs are committing these crimes. At their own risk, some Arab communities have chosen not to join the Janjaweed. But every African in Darfur is a potential victim.

---

[1] Jack Straw, 17 February 2006, "Darfur: Stop the Killing or Pay the Price," *International Herald Tribune*

[2] Report of the International Commission of Inquiry, February 2005.

The African population is too afraid to return home and plant their crops, and the international community has so far failed to provide them with adequate protection.

In January 2005, a UN International Committee of Inquiry found that crimes against humanity as heinous as genocide had taken place and that genocidal acts have probably occurred. The United States went further, identifying the crisis as genocide. Proving genocide requires proof of intent to commit genocide, and proving a government has intent to do this is very difficult.

It is clear, however, that the crisis in Darfur is genocidal; people are being systematically killed because of who they are. The systematic nature of the destructive campaign carried out by the airforce implies Government coordination at least. It is also important to note that the 1948 UN Genocide Convention requires nations to 'prevent and punish' genocide, so proof of genocide occurring is not needed before intervention can take place.

Governments now recognise that we should not be fixated by the term 'genocide'. In September 2005, the World Summit in New York recognised the 'Responsibility to Protect' people at risk of mass atrocities, whether it is called genocide, crimes against humanity or war crimes.

The Darfur Peace Agreement signed in April 2006 has been a failure. Of the three rebel groups who negotiated the peace deal, only one has signed up to it. It is widely regarded not to address the economic and political exclusion of Darfur. Moreover, the Sudanese Government has not restricted militia activity to the areas defined by the peace deal and insecurity continues. Rebel groups have become factionalised.

The crisis has now spread into Chad and the Central African Republic where armed groups supported by Sudan have attacked African villages. A UN Resolution passed in September 2006 authorised a UN force for the region. However,

Sudan has refused to accept any UN troops in Darfur and the force has not been sent.

People are more vulnerable now than ever – congregated in IDP and refugee camps. Carnage on the scale of the Rwandan genocide could easily occur if there is no protection for civilians.

Dr James Smith, Chief Executive, Aegis Trust
April 2007

CONTENTS

MANY MEN'S WIFE
Amy Evans 1

BILAD AL-SUDAN
Juliet Alicia Gilkes 15

WORDS WORDS WORDS
Jennifer Farmer 25

SILHOUETTE
Carlo Gébler 35

DISTANT VIOLENCE
Michael Bhim 53

IDP
Winsome Pinnock 75

GIVE, AGAIN?
Lynn Nottage 87

MANY MEN'S WIFE

MANY MEN'S WIFE

Amy Evans

inspired by the documentary film
All About Darfur
by Taghreed Elsanhouri

MANY MEN'S WIFE was first performed at the Tricycle Theatre, London on 24th October 2006, as part of *How Long is Never? Darfur – a response*. The play was directed by Nicholas Kent, and the cast was as follows:

RAKIM	Obi Abili
JOSEPH	Karl Collins
ASHA	Jenny Jules
LEO	Chris Tummings

Set designed by Polly Sullivan

Costumes designed by Sydney Florence

Lighting design by Darren Murray

Sound design by Paul Kizintas

CHARACTERS

ASHA	Female, owner of a marketplace stall, late twenties
JOSEPH	Male, unemployed, mid thirties
RAKIM	Male, unemployed, late twenties
LEO	Male, unemployed, mid forties

SETTING

A small town north of Khartoum. A sleepy marketplace in the center of town.

TIME

The present.

MANY MEN'S WIFE

Mid-morning. ASHA's *stall.* ASHA *rummages around, preparing for the day. From her stall, she barely makes a living peddling tea, coffee, bottled water and soda. Surrounding her stall are folding chairs and/or crates covered with pillows for customers to sit on.*

JOSEPH *reclines in one of the folding chairs. He is a man in his mid-thirties and, like the other regulars at* ASHA's *stall, he is unemployed. He holds a cup of tea in his hand and watches* ASHA *work.* ASHA *is aware of him, but does not speak to him; his presence there is as much a fixture as the chairs themselves.*

Silence.

Eventually ASHA *moves in his direction. Wordlessly she takes the empty cup from his hands and replaces it with a fresh one. He nods his gratitude.* ASHA *smiles and continues to work.*

JOSEPH	I'm not bad to look at. I don't gamble or drink. And I'm loyal. Have you ever seen me buy anything from another stall?
	(ASHA *laughs.* RAKIM *enters.*)
RAKIM	Every time I see you here, you're crooning your own praises.
JOSEPH	These are *facts*, not praises!
	(ASHA *laughs and hands* RAKIM *a steaming cup, which he gratefully accepts.*)
RAKIM	Good morning, Asha. Another bustling day at the market. If you close your eyes and listen, you can imagine the coins changing hands. Or was that the jingle of your laughter, Asha?
JOSEPH	That's the rattling in your brain. You should have it checked.

RAKIM	It sounds like bells. I bet Asha used to wear bells. And they jingled when she moved and that's how she got the idea to open a stall at the market. So she could listen to that sound forever.
JOSEPH	And look what happened. She ended up with us.
RAKIM	But we're part of the business. Aren't we, Asha? We're an indispensable element of her marketing technique.
JOSEPH	What 'technique'?
RAKIM	Can I tell Joseph? Since it's been a year and he still hasn't figured it out for himself?
JOSEPH	Figured out what?

(ASHA *laughs, as* LEO *enters.*)

LEO	That the Earth does not revolve around the sun. Rather it revolves around Asha's beautiful smile.
RAKIM	Leo. I don't have the stomach to listen to an old man flirting this early in the morning . . .
LEO	Rakim. Joseph. And of course, Asha. Without you the world would be in darkness.
RAKIM	This is what happens when men become idle. They turn into poets and pollute the world with abstractions.
LEO	Who's idle?
RAKIM	Look around you. Who isn't? Except for Asha. And myself.
LEO	You think those few weeks you wasted traveling count as 'work'?

JOSEPH	Asha. Please.
	(ASHA *goes to refill* JOSEPH'S *cup.*)
RAKIM	You can't sit in one place and wait for the tide to turn. You have to walk up to the sea and pull the tide in your direction.
LEO	'Pull the tide in your direction!' Ha! Is that what you call stowing away on a freighter? Peeling potatoes, scraping away the rust?
RAKIM	Those weeks were the best of my life! I saw things I'd never dreamed of. Stars so close you could kiss them. Dolphins. Whales –
LEO	Did they pay you?
RAKIM	(*ignoring* LEO) The world is vast. The only thing holding us back is a lack of imagination.
LEO	So let's free our imaginations! Let's catapult into the ocean and turn the current like the reins on a horse. We'll scrape rust and peel potatoes all around the world and when we come back, we'll be heroes. Our prosperity will spread like a plague. (*To* ASHA.) Think of it, Asha! The market will be teeming! You'll sell tea and coffee by the barrel! And then . . . the day will come when you must choose. And gentlemen, I'll have to say goodbye to you both. But someday, when you've recovered from your loss and have lovely wives of your own, we'll all sit together and talk about the good old days –
RAKIM	And what makes you think that Asha wants you?
LEO	Asha and I are connected in ways you wouldn't understand.
RAKIM	Like what?

LEO	We're strangers. We both appreciate silence. And we're the same height.
RAKIM	Wrong. She's taller than you.
LEO	She's taller than you as well!
JOSEPH	Why don't we let Asha choose for herself?
LEO	Because we know she's much too kind. She wouldn't want to divide her family and see them go to war with each other. She'd marry all three of us if it came to that. Wouldn't you, Asha?
	(ASHA *laughs at this, long and hard. The men join in.* LEO *lifts his cup of tea in a toast.*)
	To our Asha!
JOSEPH	To Asha.
RAKIM	To Asha.
LEO	The keeper of the peace.
	(*They drink.* ASHA *refills their cups when they're done.*)
JOSEPH	Still, I'm curious. If you had the choice, Asha. Which of us would you pick?
	(ASHA *shrugs.*)
LEO	Answer freely. We won't hold it against you. Will we, gentlemen?
RAKIM	On my mother's honour. And my father's grave.
JOSEPH	On my father's, sister's and three brothers' honour, and on my mother's grave.

LEO On the honour of all my brothers and sisters, they're too many to count. And on my grandfather's honour. He's still alive, a hundred years old. Longevity, Asha. It's in my genes —

JOSEPH So, there. You have our word. Which of us is the most eligible bachelor?

(*Pause.*)

ASHA It depends on the woman you ask.

(*Beat.*)

LEO What did she say?

JOSEPH It depends on the woman.

RAKIM Oh. Yes.

LEO Of course.

(*Awkward silence.*)

RAKIM I'm about to burst.

LEO So am I.

RAKIM Joseph, will you be here when we get back?

LEO Unless a fat man in a suit and tie swoops down from the sky and offers him a job.

RAKIM Unless he charms Asha and the two run away to be married.

LEO Chances are better for the fat man in the sky.

RAKIM You don't believe in miracles?

LEO Some miracles not even God can perform.

	(LEO *and* RAKIM *disappear, laughing.* JOSEPH *looks at* ASHA. ASHA *busies herself at her stand.*)
JOSEPH	Between us, Asha. Who is your favorite?
	(*Pause.*)
	Rakim is young and pretty. Even I think he's pretty. And Leo . . . he talks like an old woman. But there's a certain charm in his babble. And his body is stronger than it looks.
	(ASHA *snickers.*)
	Or is there another candidate? Someone we've never seen? Is that why you're laughing? To keep us from killing each other? I love my friends, Asha, but you . . . there's no crime in the world I wouldn't commit for you.
	(ASHA *shrugs.* JOSEPH *searches through his pockets and finds a bracelet, a simple chain.*)
	I have something here. It belonged to my mother. I've carried it with me for years. You're the only woman I've ever offered it to. Have it. Please.
ASHA	I DON'T WANT IT!
	(*Silence.* ASHA *works.* JOSEPH *stands still, stunned. He looks around in disbelief to see whether anyone else has seen or heard. Then he turns back to* ASHA. *After a beat,* ASHA *begins to snicker again.*)
	I've had husbands. More than I can count. Sometimes four or five at once. They jumped at me from the trees and waited for me in the shadows. Sometimes they took me in a room, but mostly they didn't bother. Under the trees was good enough. In their trucks and jeeps. In a town they'd just destroyed. I fainted under

the body of one only to wake up under the
body of another. Several times I was pregnant.
I killed the babies while they were still inside
me. What are you looking at? You and your
honour. Your sister's honour, your father's
honour, your brother's honour and your
mother's grave! For a year you've been coming
here. You never asked where I came from. You
think because I'm a stranger, I must have
walked out of the sea just so I could serve you
tea and laugh when you tried to pay me. You
were wrong. I come from Darfur. That doesn't
mean anything to you, does it? I might as well
be from the centre of the sun.

(*Pause.*)

They slaughtered my family in front of my
eyes. One by one they were pushed in a pit and
the men gathered around the edge and shot
them as they fell. They threw me in on top of
the pile, but one of the men shouted for them
to stop. 'Wait,' he said, like that. I'll never
forget his face.

(*Long pause.* ASHA *works.*)

JOSEPH   I don't know what to say.

(ASHA *snickers bitterly.*)

You must tell them. You must –

(ASHA *laughs again.* RAKIM *and* LEO *return.*)

LEO   I have sad news to report: our brother Rakim is
leaving us. He has decided to move to America,
where his can-do spirit will be better
appreciated! Rakim – I wish you well. No matter
what happens, you'll always be my little
brother –

RAKIM   You talk too much, old man. And you twist my
words around. I didn't say anything about

	going to America. I was just speculating on what would happen if the Americans came here.
LEO	What would happen?
RAKIM	Things might change.
LEO	Like what?
RAKIM	An end to conflict. Jobs, opportunities . . .
LEO	Wait! There's something . . . wipe your nose. Okay, it's gone. I think it was a little bit of your imagination hanging out.
RAKIM	I was talking about sales technique! Like Asha. Have you ever wondered why she lets us drink our tea for free? Because she's a clever, cunning woman, more than any of us will ever be. She does it to keep us coming. To make it look as if her stall is full, even in a market as deserted as this one. So people will see and say to themselves, 'Look at that. The economy is in shreds and that little stall is bursting at the seams. How does she do it? Look at the crowd gathered there. They can't tear themselves away.' Little did she know we'd fall in love and become her family. But that's what happens. Ambition breeds loyalty, and with loyalty comes love. And we need more of it here in this place. Joseph agrees with me. Don't you, Joseph?
LEO	You watch too much television, Rakim.
RAKIM	I'm talking to Joseph!
	(*Silence, while* RAKIM *waits for a response.* JOSEPH *throughout their dialogue keeps his eyes on* ASHA. ASHA *works.*)
	Joseph?

(RAKIM *and* LEO *look at each other. They see that something's wrong.*)

Joseph?

LEO Joseph? What's wrong?

(*Silently* JOSEPH *pulls up a chair and sits down before* ASHA. RAKIM *and* LEO *first look at each other and then look at him.*)

JOSEPH Listen to Asha.

(ASHA *looks up at* JOSEPH *angrily, then goes back to her work.* JOSEPH *sits patiently. After a beat, the other two sit down as well. They wait.* ASHA *continues to work in silence.*)

(*Blackout.*)

BILAD AL-SUDAN

BILAD AL-SUDAN

Juliet Alicia Gilkes

BILAD AL-SUDAN was first performed at the Tricycle Theatre, London, on 25th October 2006, as part of *How Long is Never? Darfur – a response*. The play was directed by Charlotte Westenra and the cast was as follows:

HALIMA   Funlola Olufunwa

MARIAM   Clare Perkins

During subsequent performances of BILAD AL-SUDAN, the cast was as follows:

HALIMA   Clare Perkins

MARIAM   Alibe Parsons

Set designed by Polly Sullivan

Costumes designed by Syndey Florence

Lighting design by Darren Murray

Sound design by Paul Kizintas

SETTING

A Sudanese Refugee Camp near the border with Chad. Dirt and junk homes fill the dusty expanse as far as the eyes can see.

CHARACTERS

HALIMA   In her mid-teens. Recently arrived at the Camp with her aunt. Of the Zaghawa Clan.

MARIAM   In her thirties. Several weeks at the Camp with her baby. Of the Fur Clan.

BILAL AL-SUDAN

The refugee camp. HALIMA *squats, perspiring in the hot midday sun.*

HALIMA　　As always he sits there. Picking meat from his teeth. Legs spread apart like a dog airing its testicles. Everyone calls him the 'Boss-man'. We remind the 'Boss-man' we have walked from far and search his face for pity. The response is as always: (*Halima mimics Boss-man.*) 'Who are you?' 'Are your names on the List? Show me your bracelets?' Of course we do not have any.

To get a bracelet you have to be on the List. When your name is on the List you get a bracelet. When you wear the bracelet they bring you food to last three weeks. Two cups of maize. Half a cup of cooking oil. A bag of sugar and half a bar of soap. We protest our extreme hunger. (HALIMA *mimics Boss-man.*)

'How do I know you are not locals looking for a free hand out? Spontaneous arrivals must wait two weeks! When your registration is complete you will each receive a bracelet. If you are legitimate!' (HALIMA *kisses her teeth.*)

They keep calling us the 'spontaneous ones'. But how else does one arrive in hell except spontaneously! This is not something to be planned unless you are mad or very bad. We have been waiting spontaneously for one whole week now. In another we will be dead. What use is a bracelet on a stone dead corpse? (*Pause.*) There is a rumour that our heroic Leader is coming to visit the camp. I am glad. He will show this 'Boss-man' the meaning of spontaneous. A spontaneous beating perhaps, to teach him humility. If I were a man I would beat him myself. Men folk are gathering to greet the brave fighter. He is a Zaghawa like ourselves. But Aunt Fatima does not think we should hang around to find out if this is true or not. She says there is a bad tension in the air like the gathering of thunder clouds. (*Pause.*) I try to ignore the stink rising from the dirt, junk and straw of our decaying shelter. An ugly envy stabs my belly when I see a girl resting across from me wearing a plastic bracelet. Through the layer of dust on my face I force a smile. She looks at me as if she were saying –

MARIAM (*watching* HALIMA) What does she want? Is she smiling at my baby? I turn my back. Even so I feel her eyes on me. I feel her hunger but do not recognise her kind. (MARIAM *cradles her baby.*) She speaks a foreign tongue. So many tongues here. So many faces. Fur, Zaghawa, I have even seen Masaleet. They say the Masaleet are tough and like to create trouble. Or is it the Zaghawa? We Fur like to keep to ourselves. Or so they say. It seems everybody has a quarrel now but nobody can really remember why. My Grandfather once told me how when the Earth began to dry and the soil blew away in clouds of red dust, strange Arab men came to water their camels. Well, Grandfather gathered his brothers, his uncles and sons and beat them off with sticks and whips made from cow hide. One week later the strangers returned with axes and machetes. And so it continues. Now everyone is looking for a well to drink from – a place to quench the thirst – but no one can find one. And the land it continues to shrivel. Now the men folk have guns. They are everywhere. Men with guns came to our village. They took food and cattle. Then more men with guns came and burned our village. They said we were giving food to the unholy enemy. I remember that day well. I can still hear the singing and the laughter of the women and the children. The gunfire and the screaming. The sky disappeared in a cloud of flying dirt. Six members of my family and my

husband were shredded. I had to jump over
their bodies to survive. The birds never
stopped singing –

(HALIMA *looks across at* MARIAM.)

HALIMA She sticks to that baby like an ant to a mango.
Like she thinks I'll take it from her. I do not
want her crying baby. Aunt Fatima says I have
not yet learned to be a woman. I think Aunt
Fatima has become rather soft in the head. She
has forgotten the meaning of 'survival of the
fittest'. But she just looks at me. Tells me: *'In
life one starts with oneself but should never
end with oneself'*. So how else does one die
but alone? (*Pause.*) I watch a pregnant girl
nearby. I know she feels the same as me. Every
day, she spends her time searching for roots
and herbs to make the baby flush away. But it
just clings inside her belly. (*Pause.*) She
should not stray too far. Yesterday Aunt
Fatima and me – we went outside the camp,
searching for firewood. But the locals did not
like it. They chased us back to the camp with
sticks and cowhide whips. If I get the chance
I'll return and pee on their precious wood. Let
me see them make a fire out of that! I hope the
smoke will choke them –

MARIAM I can't breathe. The situation here is getting
worse and more and more confusing. The
overcrowding is unbearable. They say a new
camp will open to take in the overflow.
Yesterday a holy man came to pray among us.
*'Your agony, your fears and your tears are
known to God'*, he said. Many of the men folk
rushed forward to greet him, (*Mimicking.*) *'If
the survival of Faith requires the shedding of
more blood, then we are here to do our duty!'*
That's what they tell the holy man. I do not
understand this kind of duty. Nobody really
does. They just pretend to. I gather my
precious child in my arms and turn my back. He
is not really my child but he doesn't really

know that. I found him on a dirt road still gouged by the many convoys of the past rainy season. He was lying beside the body of his dead mother. Clinging to an empty breast. I did not recognise his kind. But I understood his crying –

(HALIMA *looks over at* MARIAM.)

HALIMA   I feel ashamed. On my hands and knees. Scratching through the dust for loose morsels spilled from sacks of relief food as a truck delivers its load. I am not alone and the competition among those of us without bracelets is fierce. There is a rumour of a peace agreement but I am too hungry to care what it means. Our heroic Leader never showed up. I can't hide my disappointment. Once again, I weep bitter tears at the feet of the 'Boss-man'. His 'people' look at me. Not with compassion. But horror. My wailing becomes so strangled he hands me a bag of sugar. I run to Aunt Fatima with my prize. But she is not pleased: *'What are we supposed to do with one bag of sugar!'* She jumps up from her straw blanket. Naked. A Holy Book clutched to her breast. She turns her wrath on a group of men folk: *'What is wrong with you cowards and dogs! How can you allow them to treat us like this? Where are your balls? How can you run when your forefathers are rotting and FORGOTTEN!'* Then Aunt Fatima took off. Racing through the camp. Like a crazed chicken that keeps going after it's had its head cut off. Spinning and wheeling out of control. Several women folk, who were able, gave chase. Aunt Fatima's sanity had finally taken flight. More than the Janjaweed – this frightened me most. (*Pause.*) You see. You have to close your mind or lose your mind. The way I closed mine when 'they' razed our village, to the ground. With their bullets and their rifles and their monstrous flying machines. (*Pause.*) When the killing was over Father told me and Aunt

Fatima to run for our lives. He refused to come with us. He wanted to stay and bury the dead in our home land. 'Bilad al-Sudan' he said. The 'Land of the Blacks' in Arabic. He was always telling me that. Father was fluent. I don't even know if he is alive or dead –

MARIAM Last night fighting broke out between the men folk. They were armed with axes and machetes. Rumours of peace have made them very angry. Some factions have agreed to sign it. Some factions have refused. Of course the camp is now split. We have turned on ourselves. The white men who bring food – frightened by the sudden violence – have evaporated once again. Even the hand of compassion gets stung when it strokes a scorpion. Would-be boy soldiers queue up to enlist amongst the quarrelling gangs. I am seriously thinking of walking back home. I am not alone. But the older, wiser grandmothers, they remind us of the Sudanese saying, *'When there is a lion can cows go to where the lion is?'* They squat with their naked grandchildren, whispering prayers at the moon. I see the way they love each other. Hold each other. There is deep love here. It makes the old men cry. (*Pause.*) A fight erupts as two factions and their weapons collide. I too try to evaporate – like the white men before me but get caught in the riot. I lose my balance. My skull. It feels. As if. Split open –

HALIMA When you are desperate you forget the dignity you know. You are even forced to forget there is dignity to be forgotten. (*Pause.*) I reach for the bracelet hanging from her dead wrist. What is the use of a bracelet on a stone dead corpse? Her baby just stares at me. I cannot bear its gaze. It makes me weep.

(*Sound of baby crying.*)

I weep for his deserted life. For all the life I see around me. Forsaken. Abandoned. Discarded like rubbish. (HALIMA *picks up the crying child.*) So I take this life instead. I take it and I hold it. Tight. I don't recognise his tribe. But that does not matter. His clan is Sudan. 'Bilad al-Sudan'. The land of the Black People. I hear Aunt Fatima's words: *'In life one always starts with oneself but should never end with oneself'.* I crawl beside her in the darkness. At least we all have each other –

(*Sound of children's laughter and play.*)

MARIAM In my sleep I hear the singing and the laughter of the place where I was born. It is the first time in a long time that my dreams have come without fear. I look across the red earth and above my empty home. Gone are the living. Just burnt bodies upturned toward the sun. They say there is a war here but where is the story of all these victims? Their ashes all blown away. I know a crime was committed here but there's nothing left to betray, except my memory now fading. I no longer matter. If I ever did at all. After all, now that I am gone, will *you* remember me?

(*Lights fade to black.*)

words words words

words words words

Jennifer Farmer

WORDS WORDS WORDS was first performed at the Tricycle Theatre, London on 24th October 2006, as part of *How Long is Never? Darfur – a response*. The play was directed by Nicholas Kent, and the cast was as follows:

KOFI ANNAN	Chris Tummings
PEACEKEEPER	Howard Ward
AID WORKER	Clare Perkins
DOCTOR	Alibe Parsons
JOURNALIST	Obi Abili
YOUNG WOMAN	Jenny Jules

Set designed by Polly Sullivan
Costumes designed by Sydney Florence
Lighting design by Darren Murray
Sound design by Paul Kizintas

words words words

KOFI ANNAN *stands blocking a check-point which signposts the way to Darfur. He has a pencil and is trying to complete a crossword puzzle in a newspaper.*

ANNAN Eight letters . . .

(He puts his pencil in his mouth as he thinks.)

S-L-A; no, slaughter's nine. Come on, Kofi.

(An armed UN PEACEKEEPER *enters. He tries to get past* ANNAN, *but finds that his way is blocked.)*

PEACEKEEPER Excuse me, Mr Annan.

*(*ANNAN *continues to concentrate on his puzzle, so instinctively moves over, but only just slightly. He is still blocking the way, so the* PEACEKEEPER *tries to squeeze through.)*

I . . . Sorry, I can't get – Mr Annan?

ANNAN Hmmm?

*(*ANNAN *looks up from his crossword puzzle.)*

Sorry.

(He moves over a bit more, so that the PEACEKEEPER *can pass through the check-point. The* PEACEKEEPER *starts making his way through, but sees that* ANNAN's *thoughts are elsewhere.)*

PEACEKEEPER You alright, Mr Annan?

*(*ANNAN *points at the crossword puzzle.)*

ANNAN Completely stumped.

PEACEKEEPER	Maybe I can help. Pretty good at these. Won a pen for completing the *Sunday Times* crossword.
ANNAN	Be my guest.

(*He shows the* PEACEKEEPER *the puzzle. They both read the clue to themselves.*)

PEACEKEEPER	How many letters?
ANNAN	Eight.
PEACEKEEPER	Eight. (*Beat.*) War crimes? No, that's nine. War crime – singular. War crime. That's eight.
ANNAN	Yeah, but eight over two words. One eight-letter word.
PEACEKEEPER	Of course. Let's have a look again.

(*They both look at the clue again, then rack their brains. Both men shrug.*)

ANNAN	Difficult, I know.
PEACEKEEPER	I'll be damned.
ANNAN	I know.

(*An* AID WORKER *enters, carrying a box of relief supplies. She tries to get past* ANNAN *and the* PEACEKEEPER.)

AID WORKER	Excuse me, gentlemen.
PEACEKEEPER	Bloodbath?
AID WORKER	Pardon?
ANNAN	That's what I thought, but bloodbath's still nine letters.
PEACEKEEPER	Try blood with just one 'o' then. Blodbath . . .

(ANNAN *gives him look.*)

Sorry.

(*The* AID WORKER *clears her throat.*)

AID WORKER   Gentlemen, this box is rather heavy.

(*They finally look up from the puzzle.*)

PEACEKEEPER   Sorry. Scootch over, Kofi.

(*Both men shuffle over a tiny bit. The* AID WORKER *still can't get through the checkpoint. The* PEACEKEEPER *looks at the* AID WORKER.)

You look clever. (*To* ANNAN.) Doesn't she look clever?

AID WORKER   Er, thanks.

PEACEKEEPER   Are you good with words?

AID WORKER   I have been known to turn a phrase or two.

ANNAN   Have you now?

(*The* AID WORKER *shrugs with a false modesty.*)

How's this one for you. 'The systematic killing –'

AID WORKER   Decimation? Elimination? Assassination? (*Beat.*) How many letters?

ANNAN/
PEACEKEEPER   Eight.

AID WORKER   Eight. (*To herself.*) 'The systematic killing . . .'

(*Both* ANNAN *and the* PEACEKEEPER *look on hopefully.*)

Abuses of international humanitarian law?

(*The* PEACEKEEPER *starts to count the letters and both* ANNAN *and the* AID WORKER *cut him a look.*)

That was a joke.

PEACEKEEPER   Oh.

AID WORKER   Just eight letters; that is hard.

ANNAN   See?

AID WORKER   Carnage. Carnage is a good one, but that's seven.

ANNAN   Carnage is a good one. I'll save it for later.

(ANNAN *makes a note of the word on his newspaper.*)

AID WORKER   Eight letters . . . let me think.

(*All three are lost in thought. A* DOCTOR *with Medecins Sans Frontieres enters, followed by a* JOURNALIST.)

DOCTOR   Is this the way to Darfur?

(*Absentmindedly,* ANNAN, *the* PEACEKEEPER *and the* AID WORKER *all nod. The* DOCTOR *and the* JOURNALIST *both try to squeeze past the three blocking the entrance to the check-point.*)

JOURNALIST   Excuse us.

DOCTOR   I love a good crossword. I find them very relaxing.

AID WORKER   I can't come up with anything.

ANNAN	Me either. Only one thing to do: break out a thesaurus! Anybody got a thesaurus?!

(*Everyone in the queue checks all over their person, but come up empty-handed.*)

JOURNALIST	Try this.

(*Silence. Everyone is waiting.*)

Saturnalia of blood.

(*Beat.*)

ANNAN	Saturnalia of blood?
AID WORKER	Nice phrase.
JOURNALIST	Thanks.
ANNAN	It is good.
PEACEKEEPER	Bit long, though.
JOURNALIST	Can you even spell saturnalia?
PEACEKEEPER	I can spell –
JOURNALIST	Do it, then –
ANNAN	Quiet you two.
DOCTOR	Massacre. Try massacre.
AID WORKER	Massacre; that's eight.

(ANNAN *checks the crossword. Everyone looks on expectantly. Beat.* ANNAN *shakes his head.*)

ANNAN	Must start with a 'g'.

(*Everyone groans in disappointment. A* YOUNG WOMAN *enters from the other side of the check-*

point, exiting Darfur. She can't get through with all the others blocking the way. She sees that they are engrossed in the crossword puzzle, so she has a look.)

YOUNG WOMAN 'The systematic killing of all the people from a national, ethnic or religious group.' Eight letters.

ANNAN Eight.

AID WORKER Starts with 'g'.

YOUNG WOMAN Starts with 'g'. Genocide.

JOURNALIST Genocide?!

ANNAN Be quiet!

PEACEKEEPER She said genocide!

ANNAN Ssh!

YOUNG WOMAN What?

ANNAN You just used the 'g' word!

YOUNG WOMAN 'G' word? I said –

PEACEKEEPER We know what you said. And that's a word we just don't use.

YOUNG WOMAN Why not?

ANNAN You can't just go throwing that word around! We can't use that word!

YOUNG WOMAN What's wrong with calling it what it is? Genocide.

PEACEKEEPER Because . . .

JOURNALIST Because . . .

ANNAN Because then we'd have to do something.

(*Lights fade.*)

SILHOUETTE

SILHOUETTE

Carlo Gébler

SILHOUETTE was first performed at the Tricycle Theatre, London, on 24th October 2006, as part of *How Long is Never? Darfur – a response*. The play was directed by Nicolas Kent, and the cast was as follows:

REBECCA, a nurse, Irish   Charlotte Lucas

MARIAM, an IDP, Darfuri   Lorraine Burroughs

Designed by Polly Sullivan
Costumes designed by Sydney Florence
Lighting design by Darren Murray
Sound design by Paul Kizintas

SILHOUETTE was commissioned by the Tricycle Theatre, London, with help from Bloomberg LP.

THE TIME: A scorching summer in the recent past.
THE PLACE: An improvised hospital in Darfur.

SILHOUETTE

Mariam *in bed.* Rebecca *beside her.* Rebecca *has a bowl of sorghum and a spoon. There is a glass of pink hibiscus* (karkadeh) *juice on a table.*

Rebecca   Are we any better today?

(Mariam *shakes her head.*)

Well, we won't get better unless we eat, you know. Come on, open the mouth . . .

(Rebecca *feeds* Mariam *a spoon of sorghum.*)

That was easy, wasn't it? Try another. Good. So, what do you remember? Anything? Nothing? I'll tell you my side, shall I? That might jog the old memory. I was in the Land Rover, yesterday, coming here, when the driver said, 'Look' and I saw them . . . on their camels, in the distance. They were Janjaweed, weren't they? Another one? Then you stood up, I saw you, for a second, and then you fell down. We drove over. I wouldn't let the driver get out, you know. I wouldn't let him see you without any clothes on. Another? Good. I got the water can, the Wet Wipes, I cleaned you up, got you dressed. Then we put you in the Land Rover and set off. Remember that, driving here? I held your hand. 'I am Rebecca', I said. Remember? I asked your name. At first you couldn't say, but in the end you did. 'Mariam', you said, your only word. Mariam, lovely, lovely name.

(*Pause.*)

Mariam, you must talk. Try and talk to me. We can talk about anything but if we can talk about . . . Go on, take another mouthful. Excellent. Look, what happened to you has happened to hundreds, thousands of women, and there are many more who won't come forward . . . that's the stigma of course. But you can support one another, you and all those others, can't you? Another spoon? There we go. Once we got you here you were sedated and obviously we had to check in case of bleeding or . . . there was some tearing . . . a dozen stitches did it . . . Anyway . . . about what happened to you, Mariam . . . there are going to be an awful lot of women here who won't be what men want, but they'll be the only women to pick from, so the men are just going to have to get used to it . . . And they will, people adapt, even men. Here, another mouthful, there we go. Goodness. The bowl's cleared. Well done. Excellent.

(REBECCA *stands and walks away with the bowl.*)

MARIAM Silhouette.

REBECCA (*turning*) Silhouette. You said silhouette. You see a silhouette, don't you?

MARIAM Silhouette.

(*Pause.*)

REBECCA When I came up to you yesterday, the sun was behind me. Am I silhouette?

MARIAM It is hot.

REBECCA It is hot, very good, now tell me, what do you see?

MARIAM The sky . . .

REBECCA Yesterday's sky?

MARIAM Blue.

REBECCA The sky is blue, yes, with cloud wisps far away.

MARIAM   Blue sky . . .

REBECCA   Is that what you see when you look up . . . from the ground?

MARIAM   Silhouette.

REBECCA   Oh, this is excellent. This is real progress.

MARIAM   I say I am collecting firewood. Oh my stupidity, my stupidity. Why did I go out? He says to get up on his camel and he'll take me back to the camp. (*Pause.*) I am 'Girl'. I am 'Black girl'. This is what he calls me. It should have been 'Idiot', the 'Idiot who went out'. (*Pause.*) There are two others but only this one does the talking. He's the leader.

REBECCA   So these are the three I see getting on camels?

MARIAM   I have less sense than a stone. To go out, foraging. The Janjaweed haven't been round for weeks and therefore I think we'll be safe? But we aren't, we aren't, we aren't, are we? (*Pause.*) I am right beside him, he is high above me. And he is very dark against the sky.

REBECCA   Ah, *he's* the silhouette.

MARIAM   His face is covered. He wears flip flops. I remember hair on his big toe. Very black and stiff. Like thorns.

REBECCA   That would have been in your eye line.

MARIAM   I see him, head, shoulders, against the blue sky, then I see his foot, and then I see him against the sky again. Then his camel coughs. (*Pause.*) I'm getting firewood, I say. I'm getting firewood. (*Pause.*) I am from IDP camp, I say. I point in this direction.

REBECCA He would have known that anyway, wouldn't he? Or guessed it?

MARIAM 'Get up', he says again. He will take me back here. 'I have to get wood', I say, 'So no, I can't'. I think, I'll walk away. I'll walk away. I walk away. He calls. After me. What am I carrying? I say nothing. He says, 'What are you carrying?' I say nothing. He says, stop or he'll shoot. I think, I'll just walk on. Slowly. Like I haven't heard. I'll keep walking until I've vanished. Into the sky. He couldn't. He wouldn't shoot. Then a single shot. Over my shoulder. (*Pause.*) What a fool, what a fool, what a fool I am to do this, to go out, mad, stupid, stupid. I could have cooked at someone else's fire. Or else better to starve than to leave here and go out there.

REBECCA Why so hard on yourself? Without firewood you don't eat. And now he's fired you must stop. Of course you must.

MARIAM No, I must because I am not alone. Warm brown ball of flesh, bundled here, against my breast.

REBECCA A child . . . your . . . ?

MARIAM Yes.

REBECCA When we brought you in you were alone but . . .

MARIAM (*tearfully*) Three years old. They took him when they rode away.

REBECCA (*improvising*) A terrible thing, to take a child, but . . . he's not dead . . . and think, the future, it'll be . . . he'll have . . . it'll be better than . . . a mother could have ever given him.

MARIAM What?

REBECCA	Better than a mother could do, any mother, no mother, here, with a child, could give the child . . . obviously, these conditions, this camp . . .
MARIAM	Who?
REBECCA	Who? The mother.
MARIAM	Whose mother.
REBECCA	His . . . you . . . he'll have a better life than you could give him here . . .
MARIAM	Me?
REBECCA	Yes. You.
MARIAM	His mother . . .
REBECCA	Yes.
MARIAM	His mother is dead.
REBECCA	What . . .
MARIAM	My mother is dead.
REBECCA	Oh.
MARIAM	His father is dead. My father is dead. His brothers and sisters are dead. His uncles and aunts are dead. His nephews and nieces are dead. They are all dead.
REBECCA	Ah, I see.
MARIAM	They come, the Janjaweed, they come to my village. It is night. They are on camel and horseback. They put everything on fire. Everyone runs from their huts. Shooting, shooting, killing, killing. I put Abdullah down. I lie over him. I tell him, 'Stay still. Play dead.' It works. They don't touch us and in the

morning they're gone. I am his sister.
Abdullah is my brother. He is the future.

REBECCA Okay, right, and that happens . . . before you come here?

MARIAM Yes.

REBECCA With your brother?

MARIAM We walk, eighteen days . . . here.

REBECCA And then . . . yesterday?

MARIAM Yesterday? I do what I should never have done. I go out.

REBECCA Okay, but you have to. What I want to know is, at this point in what you've been telling me, as you walk off, does Abdullah cry out, so the silhouette thinks, Ah, she's got a child. I'll fire a shot, and she'll stop. Is that right?

MARIAM Yes . . . maybe . . . bang! The next bullet will be in my head. The silhouette shouts that after me too. So of course I don't run. I stop. Stupid . . .

REBECCA We've been over this. It is pointless to feel guilt when you've no choice and you're made to do something.

MARIAM Clip, clop, clip, clop.

REBECCA That's his camel coming after you?

MARIAM He comes up. Biz, biz, biz, biz.

REBECCA What's that?

MARIAM The silhouette, he's talking, shush.

REBECCA And what do you say back?

MARIAM	Biz, biz, biz, biz.
REBECCA	Meaning?
MARIAM	They get down then, the three of them and you know what these devils do to young girls. We are black, we are ripe and they eat us. The other two take all my clothes and push me down. Very hot the ground and stony and he, the silhouette, he smells of mutton fat. And petrol. He smells of gun oil. And camel. And leather. And old sweat. And . . .

(*Pause.*)

REBECCA	And where is your brother now?
MARIAM	I don't know.
REBECCA	Do you hear him crying maybe? He is alive, isn't he?
MARIAM	Yes.

(*Pause.*)

After the silhouette, the other two have their turn.

(REBECCA *hands* MARIAM *the glass of juice.*)

REBECCA	Here, drink some of this.

(MARIAM *takes a sip.*)

MARIAM	Then they hear your engine.
REBECCA	Why don't they run off as soon as they hear us?
MARIAM	They are too busy. They hear you when the third is . . . 'Oh, NGO people', says the silhouette. 'We'll kill them', he says. 'We'll take the Land Rover'. But then, he says no.

'No, we won't kill them', he says. 'We've finished here'. He picks up Abdullah. (*Pause.*) I am an idiot to believe he'd keep his word.

REBECCA   Well, he's Janjaweed, what do you expect?

MARIAM   The camels kneel and they get up and they go off.

REBECCA   I see that and then I see you standing, amidst the thorn bushes and then you fall, and we drive up. You're breathing and your eyes are open.

MARIAM   I think you are an angel.

REBECCA   If only.

MARIAM   I mean at first. Then I know you aren't. Your smell. Not like them but a smell all the same. You smell white.

(*Pause.*)

REBECCA   Talking helps, don't you think? Have another drink. You've got to get your fluids in.

(MARIAM *takes another sip of juice.*)

REBECCA   After the silhouette fires the shot and catches up with you again, what does he say?

MARIAM   Biz, biz, biz, biz.

REBECCA   What is that? What is he saying?

MARIAM   Shush. The silhouette is speaking.

REBECCA   What is he saying?

MARIAM   Biz, biz, biz, biz.

REBECCA   You're talking too, though? What are you saying?

MARIAM	Shush.
REBECCA	It's about your brother isn't it?
MARIAM	No. Shush.
REBECCA	Yes. The Janjaweed are slavers and you've got a child. We have the statistics. They take them all the time. In Khartoum, placed with a good family, they can get several hundred dollars, a fortune, for a strong healthy black child like your brother.
MARIAM	Biz, biz, biz, biz. Shush.
REBECCA	But it isn't the worst. The worst is he's dead and he's not. He's going to be slaved, and that's got to be better. This means the silhouette will look after him properly because he'll want to sell him for a good price. (*Pause.*) This means who ever buys him, they'll look after him because if they do, they can get twenty or thirty years work out of him. (*Pause.*) And this means we can find him. Yes, we can. (*Pause.*) He could be in Khartoum already. Or on his way to Saudi. Maybe not. (*Pause.*) Anyway, he'll be easy to find. How many families have a black child slave?
MARIAM	Don't say that word.
REBECCA	Okay, who's an unpaid servant and comes from Darfur? How many? We'll get him back and with DNA testing we'll prove you're related, easy.
MARIAM	You will never find him.
REBECCA	What do you mean? I'd say there's a very good chance we'll get him, really.
MARIAM	No, never.

REBECCA	Well, we've got to try at least. We have contacts, there are agencies, Sudan's not completely impossible.
MARIAM	I don't want to try.
REBECCA	You don't want to try? You know your problem. Guilt. 'I should never have gone for firewood.' You think your brother will blame you for that? No. You had to go out. Plus, as I keep saying, dead is worse and he's not dead. We can find him.
MARIAM	No.
REBECCA	You don't know.
MARIAM	I do know.
REBECCA	So you wouldn't consider looking?
MARIAM	No.
REBECCA	Why not? Give me one good reason.
MARIAM	I need to walk into the sky, to become invisible.
REBECCA	That's not a reason.
MARIAM	I don't want to, and if I don't want to, then I don't have to.
REBECCA	Now you're stamping your foot . . . like a child. (*Pause.*) Just saying no, just saying no, over and over and over again, I don't understand. (*Pause.*) Look, we've all got a little secret. (*Pause.*) I'm ashamed of things I've done. Everyone has a secret. You have a secret, too.
MARIAM	No. I have not. I have no secret. None. Fools don't.
REBECCA	You gave him up, didn't you? You said, take him, leave me.

MARIAM	What? You think this is what I am like? You are disgusting.
REBECCA	I'm just trying to establish the truth, get it out, into the light, so you can move on . . .
MARIAM	You know nothing. Nothing. You only come after. You only know about blood and dirt. You clean me up. You dress me. You drive me here. But for the rest, what happened before, actually, you know less than nothing.
REBECCA	Excuse me, I do know this. Trauma must be faced or you go mad and the first step is to get it in perspective. Nothing, nothing is your fault. Understand? You have to offer your brother up. You have no choice. And it's been happening in Sudan since slaving started. Women have always sold their children to give those children a better chance. But you don't get money. You get a promise from the silhouette that he and the other two won't dirty you and make you unmarriageable. And you believe them. For a moment. But then, because the Janjaweed are mad, callous, bastards, they break their word, which is typical . . . they take you *and* they take Abdullah. (*Silence.*) Why aren't you talking? Why aren't you saying something? (*Pause.*) I have been very brutal. I could have done that in a completely different way. I'm sorry. I really am.
	(REBECCA *notices* MARIAM'S *unfinished glass of juice.*)
	Do you want something else to drink?
MARIAM	No.
REBECCA	We've got some cold Fanta, it's Libyan, it's too sweet but it's better than your hibiscus juice. I'm having one.

MARIAM	Nothing, thank you.

(REBECCA *goes off, returns with a can of Fanta and opens it.*)

REBECCA	You've got to stop being so hard on yourself. I would have done the same as you. I would.

(REBECCA *drinks.*)

MARIAM	Do you think I would give my brother up?
REBECCA	Yes, and I'd have done it too, didn't you hear me?
MARIAM	But my brother?
REBECCA	Yes, I'd have traded my brother.
MARIAM	You can't see?
REBECCA	What else can it be? You're weak, they have guns. So you make an arrangement. That's what's this biz, biz, biz, biz is about. It's you talking. And you're ashamed now, which is why you won't even consider looking for your brother.
MARIAM	You don't see, do you?
REBECCA	I don't? I think I do.
MARIAM	If I make an arrangement . . .
REBECCA	Yes.
MARIAM	Why assume I make a swap, him for me?
REBECCA	What else could you have done? What other arrangement is there?
MARIAM	Me for him.
REBECCA	You.

MARIAM	Me for him, *me and I keep him*, but then, don't you see, then . . . |//

MARIAM: Me for him, *me and I keep him*, but then, don't you see, then . . .

(*Pause.*)

There is hope for a while, I have it. I have hope when I stare up at the sky . . . I am ruined but I will keep my brother. But, then, he picks up Abdullah and the camels kneel and they get up and they go off.

(MARIAM *smashes her glass on the floor and begins to cry.*)

He breaks his word and he picks up Abdullah and the camels kneel and they get up and go off.

REBECCA: Oh Lord, I'm so sorry. Me and my mouth, me and my mouth.

(REBECCA *reaches forward.* MARIAM *shakes her head and shoos her away.*)

MARIAM: Every promise broken, every single one, from the start, from as far back as I can remember, from the moment I started to remember, those devils on camels broke every promise, every last one. Why did I think he'd stick to what he'd agreed? I should have run, done . . . anything, but I didn't. I believed when he gave his word. This is my failure. How could I tell my brother I am so stupid? How? Tell me, you who knows everything, how?

REBECCA: Please, I'm so sorry, me and my bloody mouth.

MARIAM: I am the cunt of a cow neither meat nor leather, useless, useless, useless.

(*Blackout.*)

DISTANT VIOLENCE

DISTANT VIOLENCE

by Michael Bhim

DISTANT VIOLENCE was first performed at the Tricycle Theatre, London, on Tuesday 24 October 2006, as part of *How Long is Never? Darfur – a response*. The play was directed by Charlotte Westenra. The cast was as follows:

HUSBAND	Obi Abili
WIFE	Clare Perkins
JOURNALIST	Karl Collins
PHOTO-JOURNALIST	Howard Ward
REBECCA	Charlotte Lucas
DAVID	Chris Tummings

Set designed by Polly Sullivan
Costumes designed by Sydney Florence
Lighting design by Darren Murray
Sound design by Paul Kizintas

CHARACTERS

Scene One   Wife
                 Husband
                 Militiaman

Scene Two   Journalist
                 Photojournalist

Scene Three   Rebecca
                 David

SETTING

An expressive use of lighting should be used to emphasise the different locations of the three scenes. The time is present.

Scene One   The action takes place in a small village in West Darfur, just outside Deleig.

Scene Two   A militia outpost fifteen miles east of Deleig.

Scene Three   An upstairs flat in Swiss Cottage, London.

DISTANT VIOLENCE

Scene One

The sun shines brightly, almost blindingly on WIFE *as she speaks. As she speaks the sunlight should gradually dim to suggest a passage of time, from morning to early evening.*

WIFE . . . I have seen the sun, I have lay on my back and I have stared into the sun, I have had its heat make me sick . . . I have seen ropes, tied in the dust, tied to dead livestock, I have been tied to ropes, that have been anchored around the abandoned green and white mosque, the mosque which stands riddled with bullets, standing with blood pouring from black holes in its green and white walls. (*Pause.*) . . . I have seen, what is unseen, I have seen people defy the state, the state religion, I have seen inside the mosque the smell of metal, of urine, of people's last prayers, of gun smoke, of fathers and sons, of mothers and sons, rotting, lying one on top the other, fathers dumped on top of mothers, little boys lying dead, next to their plastic toys, and dead fears, and nightmares, and many questions about life, finished, stopped, irrelevant, extinguished.

I have closed my eyes, and ignored the sound of the dead that I have heard scream, those that have died in mid-explanation, mid-excuse, mid-rebuke. The angry people, the beautiful people, the confused, the embittered, the good, the giving people. I have imagined myself with wings looking down at the decapitated houses, and dreamt of planes flying to and from New York, with men looking out of their windows, men who've removed their eyes and replaced them with US dollars, holding briefcases of Sudanese gold, who get angry when you shine mirrors in their faces in case they see their own reflections, in case they see their obsessions for artificial things, for principles, for security,

for only looking out for one's self. (*Pause.*) I
have closed my eyes and I have seen them see
my dreams. Dreams of weak words that travel
from Khartoum with the promise of schools, the
promise of options, of travel. And me, I have
seen myself holding optimism, watching it burn
holes into my hands.

I can remember the sound of the water pump,
the sound of running water, of my reflection in
the water, of the feel of my arm, of its skin, its
individuality, of my wrist without the feeling of
being held, but of holding. I remember being a
child living on this land, living with a
government that protected its people, like how
my father harnessed me, it harnessed us. Now
there is silence, only the burning of skin, the
hanging of men. Now, all the houses have
bones protruding from them. While I lay on my
back. In the sun. In the heat with the other
women. Our men standing. Made to watch.
Their eyes forced open, while the sound of the
Hakama is sung. While the song of joy is sung.
And us. While we lie. Dirt forced in our
mouths. Dirt filled in our bodies . . . and where
is the government? . . . Where is my father?
Where is Al Khartoum?

(WIFE *stands in what is now almost darkness.
In the distance behind her* HUSBAND *is
standing. He has been standing there for some
time unnoticed. He props himself up with a
stick, as one of his legs is wrapped with a
bloodstained cloth. She stands with her back
to him, she refuses to look at him. They are in
their house.* HUSBAND *is holding a package. It
is an NGO food parcel.*)

HUSBAND (*sharp*) Ears are made for listening, okay! . . .
Okay? So, when I say a thing, or, or a, a sound,
those two things at the side of your face
should, should vibrate, and, automatically, that
should alert you in my direction! . . . And if
you take into account all the vibrations coming

out of my mouth, going straight to you, then I can see no reason why you keep ignorin' me!

WIFE (*calm*) I didn't hear you.

HUSBAND Oh you heard me! I don't believe that!

WIFE Then believe what you want.

HUSBAND Damn right I'll believe what I want (*Slight pause. Propping himself up with his stick.*) . . . What is it with you? Five hours . . . ? Dragging my feet in the hot sand, with the sun, the sun, burning through to my bones and for what? So that I come back to see you spending all your time daydreaming? Staring at the walls, talking to yourself?

WIFE (*self-assured*) I was not talking to myself.

HUSBAND (*sarcastically*) So I'm blind huh?

WIFE Maybe you are.

HUSBAND Oh yes that's right . . . I'm just imagining your mouth moving up and down, because all the fucking dead people I'm seeing, it's made me that confused in the head.

WIFE Maybe it has.

(*Long pause. He is about to say something but is stuck for words.*)

HUSBAND (*best attempt at being calm*) You going to eat what I got you, or you not going to eat what I got?

WIFE Just put it on the table.

HUSBAND I don't feel like putting it on the . . . (*Slight pause.*) What's it gonna take for you to look at me? (*Pause. She doesn't respond. Count of five, then a venomous outburst.*) Don't you make me come over there now!

WIFE (*suddenly turning to look at him*) What? . . . What is it? . . . There okay, you're looking at me.

(*They stare at each other. He breaks into a smile.*)

HUSBAND . . . Your forehead looks slightly different from the last time I saw it . . . first time in a week I get to see your face.

WIFE (*interrupting*) What d'you want?

HUSBAND What do I want? . . . I want normality. (*He holds out the food parcel.*) Go get some fuel, we'll cook this food I've got.

WIFE Why? They'll be back here to kill you before the morning.

HUSBAND (*slight pause*) . . . So what? (*He tries to open the parcel, but it is difficult for him.*) . . . Let them come . . . I'll welcome them . . . Let them come, with that government blood money, like they've done all over Deleig. With their government guns, like they've done to the Zaghawa. When they came here they knew we had nothing to do with the SLA, nothing! Did that stop them? (*Slight pause.*) They've been eyeing this land, ever since the droughts started . . . our land was good, we cared for our land . . . Now they starve 'cos their backward farming methods leaves their kids hungry, that is not my problem!

WIFE Telling them that is not gonna stop them trying to kill us.

HUSBAND Fuck 'em! (*He stops trying to open the parcel.*) . . . I swear, they'll have to blow my face clean off its head if they think they'll come here and fight over what scraps we have left.

WIFE And who's principles are you following?

HUSBAND Mine!

WIFE Yours?

HUSBAND Yes! Mine!

WIFE (*raising her volume to his high level*) Or the principles of every man in this village that lies dead in the streets.

HUSBAND (*flicking his hand at her in disgust*) You're a woman, I don't expect you to understand these kinda things. (*Slight pause.*) A man, a man dies for his principles. (*Slight pause.*) If not his principles, his land. (*He then continues to try and open the parcel. Unable to do so and filled with complete frustration he throws the parcel to the floor near* WIFE'S *feet.*) Fucking Dammit! (*His stick falls to the ground.*)

WIFE Why don't you stay with the Europeans, your leg's infected.

HUSBAND My leg's fine.

WIFE It's not, you need it treated.

HUSBAND (*a bark*) It's fine!

WIFE ... You'll die if you don't stay with them.

HUSBAND Then I die twice over!

WIFE What is wrong with you?

(*Pause.*)

HUSBAND What kind of woman did I marry, that she thinks it okay for me to run with arms open to these Foreigners, when their great grandfathers cut this country up with a hot knife, and allowed the nomads to migrate right through onto our land. And now they want to be our savours? And you swallow it like gold. You swallow it!

WIFE They're the only ones we can trust!

HUSBAND Well just 'cos their faces are white, don't give 'em purer hearts, you hear me? (*Slight pause.*) Everything they give is stained with the blood of my father, and his father, and his father before that. (*Pause.*) . . . Take away the natural resources of a country, and have the whole nation fight over the scraps left behind, this is what happens.

WIFE Then leave.

HUSBAND I will not leave, not Sudan.

WIFE The mosque is filled with half the village lying dead!

HUSBAND So you leave . . . Go, get out of this continent! Do like your cousins, catch a boat from Port Sudan to Europe, England, go play on the seaside like the postcards. Like you said you were going to do! Which was the only fucking reason I went to the camp! (*She turns away. Pause.*) What? You think now your life is worth nothing? You tell me about life but you can't even leave the house, you won't even look at me. (*Long pause.*) I don't see you as no less of a woman for what they've done. (*Pause.*) I just . . . (*Pause.*) You forced me to leave this morning and I listen . . . But I couldn't, I couldn't stay in a camp, with people forgetting who they are. (*Pause.*) Maybe . . . (*Pause.*) Maybe in life this is all the time we get. But if it is I refuse to have a new beginning, to scrape away my past and start all over again, this is my home, this place, my heart lies in the ground. I can't do anything about that. And if I die, at least I die with truth. I can accept that.

(*Long pause.*)

WIFE I was planning to stay here alone and let them kill me. (*Pause.*) . . . but if you go, I'll go.

HUSBAND I don't want to hear what you're saying . . .

WIFE (*talking over him*) . . . If you go I'll go with you.

HUSBAND (*he laughs, more a sign of resignation*) To be foreigners some place? Have the rest of my life without my land . . . to be at the bottom, without a language? Never . . . (*Slight pause.*) Everything I know in life, is here, you used to be a teacher, with all those kids, now look at you . . .

(*Hesitantly she slowly picks up the food parcel and walks up to him. She picks up his stick and puts it in his hand.*)

HUSBAND Why do I listen to you?

WIFE I'm smarter than you.

(*He kisses* WIFE'S *forehead. She then supports* HUSBAND *as they walk off-stage. From the distance the sound of camels and vehicles can be heard approaching, getting louder and louder.*)

HUSBAND (*quietly*) . . . Put some soil in my pocket before we go.

(*Just before they reach the exit, they both freeze.* HUSBAND *rapidly stands in front of* WIFE. *Hesitantly they stagger back on-stage. From off-stage, walking towards them is a* MILITIAMAN. *He holds a Kalashnikov rifle – a*

*Chinese variant Type-56 – pointed at them.
He aims his rifle at them and pulls back the
charge handle. Lights down.*)

Scene Two

A militia outpost fifteen miles outside the village. A Journalist, *sits at a table, rapidly flicking through a mass of papers, he is cross-referencing some information. A* Photojournalist, *mid-forties, is idly walking around. From time to time he inspects the camera that hangs around his neck.*

Journ (*looking up*) I gotta tell you . . .

Photo What now?

Journ The longer we wait the less chance we get to negotiate with them . . . Any minute, I'm sure, the SLA are gonna sign the Peace Agreement.

Photo They all ain't gonna sign it.

Journ . . . And I mean, if that happens, the raid? It'll get called off and –

Photo Hey, hey, look. The raid this *evening*? It's definitely taking place.

Journ Is it?

Photo Don't worry about it . . . (*Glancing at him.*) You'll get your story.

(*Long pause.* Journalist *observes* Photojournalist, *who again is busy inspecting the lens on his camera.* Journalist *then resumes looking through his papers. A silence.*)

Journ It's just with the amount of money, I've spent. My editor –

Photo	(*turning to him*) You know, I'll tell you something.
Journ	What?
Photo	I set out doing this when I first saw the Cambodian Killing Fields by Don McCullen, '76.
Journ	So, so what?
Photo	Now, listen . . . That's when I realised, I cared about capturing conflict, legally, illegally . . . It's what this business is about! Getting that image. (*Pause.*) So enjoy the experience. You're in Africa for God's sake.
Journ	I just want that story!
Photo	You'll get it! (*Looking through his camera.*) . . . Man I tell you, looking down right across the Sahara from a helicopter or a panoramic view of the Jebel Mountains, man what a sight. You should see it.
Journ	(*looking up from his work*) What's the greatest thing you've seen since being here?
Photo	The greatest thing? . . . Well, in twelve years . . . ?
Journ	Would be?
Photo	The mass exodus 2003. From Darfur to Chad.
Journ	. . . Right.
Photo	(*slight pause*) . . . I dunno if you still would have been in University studying when we buggered the Kurds '91, and you had them scattered on the mountains between Turkey and Iran.
Journ	I remember that, of course.

Photo	Well, it had the same impact on me. That image, it was something else.
Journ	(*referring to his papers*) You'd think that this place doesn't exist.
Photo	Darfur definitely exists, mate.
Journ	No, I know that, but . . .
	(*There is a loud banging on the door. They both look at each other.*)
Photo	(*small smile*) I'll go see about our glorious terms of passage, should I? . . . Cash? Or cheque?
	(Journalist *reluctantly dumps a wad of US dollars on the table. The* Photojournalist *grabs it and walks off-stage. The* Journalist *looks on in the same direction. Thirty seconds passes.* Photojournalist *returns, he holds a piece of paper in his hand.*)
Photo	. . . Right. (*He sees* Journalist *with his mobile in hand.*) What the hell you doing?
Journ	My editor –
Photo	Turn the damn thing off!
Journ	Why?
Photo	. . . There's enough fucking planes and bombs in the region, I wouldn't be surprised if a fucking 1.42 picked up your blasted signal and wiped us off the fucking desert!
Journ	Alright, I'll turn it off!
Photo	Jesus Christ!
Journ	I'm sorry.
Photo	Simple, simple, simple! Common sense!

JOURN Okay, alright? (*He takes his phone and angrily dismantles it, slapping it on the table.*) There okay?

(*Pause.*)

PHOTO (*wiping his forehead*) Well, okay, now look ... The terms are as follows ... They're willing to take us with them to a village they previously visited-stroke-attacked a week ago. The rules are: There will be no photographs taken of anything other than *scenery*, (scenery my arse, we'll work around that) ... Secondly, no photographs directly of the militia or any written materials that shed a negative light on their activities, (again, I mean, either you write about Alice in Wonderland or cold-blooded murder, your choice, you know?) (*Slight pause.*) Here, you need to sign it. (*He holds out the piece of paper.*)

JOURN Why?

PHOTO Well if you don't, they'll just shoot you, that's all. (*Slight pause.*) Throw you in a tub of acid.

(JOURNALIST *takes the paper and signs.*)

(*With no loss of time, they are at the village, changing into their protective gear. As they continue talking, a few metres behind them a soft light brings into view the bodies of* HUSBAND *and* WIFE, *lying on the ground, close together. A pool of blood slowly pours out from underneath them, spreading onto the floor.*)

PHOTO As it goes, I believe there's talk of a mosque in this town where a mass-execution was held.

JOURN (*instantly reaches into his pocket, pulls out a paper and scans it*) Dead SLA sympathisers.

PHOTO Well, if they say so . . .

JOURN You know anything of the Christian contingent here?

PHOTO (*suddenly serious*) The what?

JOURN The Christian . . . what? What have I said?

PHOTO Nothing, nothing at all. (*A mocking plea to himself.*) . . . I swear, you ask for a fucking sword, you get given a shit stick!

JOURN What!?

PHOTO I just figured it out. You're one of them inexperienced journalists, ain't you? out to write that dramatic story! . . . What does it matter, your people'll only keep it tucked away in whatever editing supermarket of world conflicts the media keep stashed until its politically convenient.

JOURN Look I'm just here to report, mate. I don't know what you're talking about!

PHOTO Report? (*He laughs mockingly.*)

JOURN Yes report! I've been cross-referencing streams of information for the last two days.

PHOTO What? Sitting in a five-star hotel in Khartoum where I picked you up, sipping your fucking café au lait? Gimmie a break! You're about as close to the conflict as that biased self-serving NGO pile of shit you've filled your head with.

JOURN Now look here, alright! (*Snatching at a piece of paper to read out.*) Fact! (*Reading.*) Islamic Fundamentalist, government-sponsored militia are out to suppress the majority African population.

PHOTO

And who says that? Who? . . . Christian Aid? . . . Look man, what you're planning to write is just not true, You can't just use information that you know is biased! This is a complex regional conflict. And the government? They don't give a shit, as long as they keep profiting from the Chinese. (*Slight pause.*) Half the oil in Sudan is untapped. And every other western nation is just waiting to get their hands on it! . . . Its a free for all. It's the people that are being left to die!

JOURN

So you're saying it's Muslims killing Muslims.

PHOTO

You know it is! Don't fucking play dumb with me . . . Does she not look Muslim to you? (*Slight pause.*) You know, there's a reason I opted for Woolwich Polytechnic over Cambridge . . . I tell you, some of you boys come out of that place as thick as planks, no integrity, nothing! (*Slight pause.*) . . . The world is not just black and white, you can't just separate the good from the evil!

JOURN

(*laughs, however sounding ridiculous*) I'm sorry but no news agency will give two hoots about a bunch of Muslims fighting over land in the middle of a place that frankly doesn't exist! It's just not important enough!

PHOTO

Not important enough? People are dying!

JOURN

Well if it was, you think Kofi Annan or George Clooney would still be talking their heads off to the security council? (*Slight pause.*) . . . The whole UN will agree that something should be done, but I wonder which nation will accept the burden of doing anything, especially after what happened to the Belgians in Rwanda? You idealistic photographer, this is not the 60s, this is not McCullen in Vietnam, this is now!

PHOTO

Fine, fuck it, Fuck it! Let me do what you paid me to do. What pictures do you want?

JOURN	Let's look for that emblematic image of Darfur, You know what to look for? That dramatic image.

PHOTO	The truth, it burns and withers away like every other injustice in life . . . just remember that!

JOURN	Look in the long run it'll do some good. (*Slight pause.*) Okay, okay, so look, we've got Fundamentalist Muslims killing Africans. It's simple, it's understandable . . . the David verses the Goliath, the good verses the growing evil menace. (*Pause.*) So help me get that image, the mis-en-scene, that moment in history, and all that. (*Slight pause.*) I wanna get a good story out of this.

PHOTO	(*Long pause.*) Fine. (*Slight pause.*) . . . Remove her headscarf.

JOURN	(*carefully removeing her Hijab*) Christ . . . (*Turning back*). I promise you this'll stop the killing, it has to! . . . The British people, they just need to know that death in this world is happening and it must be stopped. (*Slight pause.*) Public opinion can affect foreign policy. Why complicate the story?

PHOTO	. . . Enjoy your British Journalism Award.

JOURN	I will. I certainly will!

(PHOTOJOURNALIST *sizes up image and in a flash captures the image of the two dead bodies. Lights out, and up again on . . .*)

Scene Three

DAVID *sits at breakfast reading a newspaper. Opposite him is his girlfriend* REBECCA, *she reads a magazine. They sit in silence. Totally engrossed in her magazine* REBECCA *suddenly bursts out laughing. In annoyance* DAVID *looks over his newspaper at her angrily, until she finishes laughing. All is quiet again and* DAVID *settles himself down to resume reading his newspaper. They sit in silence. Suddenly* REBECCA *again bursts into hysterics.*

DAVID (*throwing his paper down*) Jesus, dammit woman! Can you keep your jibbering to yourself?

REBECCA Oh mind your own business.

DAVID (*picking up his paper*) They should, and I'm going to recommend they do this, ban those glossed-up wastes of paper you're reading.

REBECCA (*looking at him*) And why's that?

DAVID So no-brainers like you don't feel compelled to bring such things into nice respectable houses such as mine.

REBECCA Now Dave dear, just hush up and go and make breakfast. (*She resumes reading her magazine.*)

DAVID It's all nonsense!

REBECCA (*flapping her paper down*) Well keep nagging me and that isn't the only thing that'll stop coming into this bloody nice house of yours . . . (*Again reading.*)

(*An inaudible mumble from* DAVID.)

REBECCA And I love you too, babe. (*Long Pause. Again they continue reading in silence.*)

DAVID (*putting his paper down*) It's just, it'd make a change if you'd read something –

REBECCA (*plainly*) What – political?

DAVID No, not necessarily.

REBECCA	Or how about something that's just intellectually inclined even. Or a paper that's so huge and intimidating, that everyone on the bus can see just how smart you are.
DAVID	I'm talking about getting to know what's going on in the world. Instead of who's getting fat or who's sleeping with who.
REBECCA	Well, I already know what's going on in the world.
DAVID	You don't have a clue!
REBECCA	Look, people die here too, many, in unjust ways.
DAVID	(*geting up and dumping the paper he's reading onto* REBECCA'S *lap*) Here, take a look at this.
REBECCA	(*throwing the paper on the floor in disgust*) That's disgusting!
DAVID	(*picking the paper up*) You see?
REBECCA	What was that?
DAVID	(*standing up, reading aloud*) A Darfurian man and his wife are shot to death inside their home. . . . The latest attack from a fundamentalist Islamic government on its people.
REBECCA	Well I'm sure there's already something being done about the Middle East.
DAVID	This is not the Middle East.
REBECCA	Where is it then?
DAVID	You see . . . ? You see? And you say you already know what's going on in the world. It's in Africa, Sudan.

REBECCA	Well, it makes a change
DAVID	(*seriously*) You shouldn't say things like that.
REBECCA	(*mocking serious*) No? Oh, I'm sorry.
DAVID	I mean Becky, look . . . (*Referring to the picture.*)
REBECCA	What?
DAVID	Extremism, it's dangerous . . . we have to stop it in places such as Darfur, so it doesn't reach here. Because it will.
REBECCA	You're a voyeur.
DAVID	Oh fuck off!
REBECCA	You have nothing to complain about, but you've got all this energy. Do yourself a favour, just stop watching the news for a while, okay? Go read a magazine, a football mag.
DAVID	I'm being serious. Our government wouldn't –
REBECCA	We've bloody taken part in every march that's happened for the last couple of years! Can you for once just pull the reigns in on your enthusiasm?
DAVID	I'm going to have a look on the net to find out what action can be taken. (*Getting up and walking off-stage.*)
REBECCA	Well, fine, but just make us a cup of tea before you do, okay? (*Slight pause.*) . . . Okay?
DAVID	(*from off-stage*) Alright!
	(REBECCA *resumes reading her magazine but is compelled take a few thoughtful glances at the image in newspaper that lies on the opposite chair. Lights fade.*)

IDP

IDP

by Winsome Pinnock

IDP was first performed at the Tricycle Theatre, London on Tuesday 24th October 2006, as part of *How Long is Never? Darfur – a response*. The play was directed by Indhu Rubasingham and the cast was as follows:

IDRIS   Lorraine Burroughs

MARIAM   Clare Perkins

Designed by Polly Sullivan
Costumes designed by Sydney Florence
Lighting design by Darren Murray
Sound design by Paul Kisintas

IDP

A camp for IDPs, Darfur. Two women are on stage. MARIAM, *the older woman, carries a basket.* IDRIS *stands in front of her, barring her way.*

IDRIS   Where are you going?

MARIAM   What's it to you?

IDRIS   Tell me you are not going outside.

MARIAM   Again I say, what business is it of yours?

IDRIS   Didn't you hear that it wasn't safe to leave the camp?

MARIAM   I am not afraid so why should you be bothered? Let me pass. I must collect firewood for cooking.

     (MARIAM *tries to pass but* IDRIS *blocks her way again.*)

IDRIS   Don't you know that the Janjaweed are out there, waiting for old women like you to set foot outside?

MARIAM   They don't pay any attention to old women like me. It is the young women they're after. Women like you.

IDRIS   Women like me, eh? And what do they do to young women like me?

MARIAM   (*bowing her head, putting distance between herself and* IDRIS) I don't know. I don't know about such things.

IDRIS   Eh? What do they do to women like me? Tell me, mother.

MARIAM   I am not your mother.

IDRIS	Tell me what they do to women like me.
MARIAM	Why can't you leave me in peace? What do you want from me? Each day I turn around and there you are over my shoulder, following me like a ghost.
IDRIS	A ghost, eh? Is that how you wish to think of me?
MARIAM	Why must you bother me like this?
IDRIS	Is it easier for you to think of me as having died?
MARIAM	Why must you torture me with this talk of death every single day? Haven't we all experienced so many different kinds of hell?
IDRIS	Is that why you pretend that you cannot recognise me, you who know every mark on my body?
MARIAM	Young woman I am very sorry that you have lost your mother, but haven't we all lost so much? Look at me: am I not too old to be your mother? Now, if you called me grandmother I could possibly understand but . . .
IDRIS	Oh my dear mother. Why didn't I see it before? I thought that you were playing a cruel game with me, but now I see that you have a sickness of the mind. All memory has gone from you.
MARIAM	I may be old but my memory is as sharp as a young girl's. I remember everything as though it were yesterday.
IDRIS	So why don't you recognise me? You, who couldn't bear to let me out of your sight. Look, (*She bares her arm.*) That was when I fell

out of a tree. (*She indicates her forehead.*) And this was when I threw myself out of your arms when I was a tiny infant. Of course I can't remember it but you, you remember. You used to read me those scars like stories in a book.

MARIAM   I cannot read the stories written on your body because they are written in a language that I do not understand.

IDRIS   Not to mention the way you used to read my thoughts. No matter how hard I tried to arrange my face to put you off the scent you only had to look at me to know what was going on in my mind – whether I was happy or sad . . .

MARIAM   I am very sorry but you are a complete stranger. Of course I understand why you would make believe a mother for yourself; but we are all in the same boat here – we have all, all of us lost everything – family, children, home – everything.

IDRIS   Why do you pretend not to recognise me, your own daughter? I have never needed your love more than I do right now. Are you ashamed? Still? That's what it is isn't it, mother? You're ashamed. It is the new scars that you refuse to read, isn't it mother?

(*The lights change.* IDRIS *and* MARIAM *speak out directly to the audience.*)

IDRIS   My mother was already old when she gave birth to me. She says that, although I was a miracle, my birth – in her mature years – set her apart from other mothers in the same way that the barrenness of her youth had marked her out. As a young woman the other mothers viewed her childlessness as a sign of God's displeasure and her big pregnant belly, at an age when most of them had completed the menopause, as further proof of such. To her

	however I was nothing but a blessing, a bundle of total joy.
MARIAM	Yes, you are right. I had a daughter, a daughter I loved far more than any woman has a right to indulge a child.
IDRIS	My father? Oh, he disappeared one night. Just like that. Went out to collect firewood and never came back. Gone in a puff of smoke. These days you come to expect such things.
MARIAM	This complete love made her fearless, tough as any boy. If I had been less indulgent perhaps things would have turned out differently.
IDRIS	Not that I minded it with just the two of us. It's a terrible thing to say, but his presence had meant that she had less time for me. Not that I had wished for him to disappear. Of course not.
MARIAM	Then there was the time of the big questions – why this? Why that? A multitude of questions – why do we live this way? Why is there nothing to eat? With a bright child like that there is no point in making things up.
IDRIS	They were telling women to stay inside after dark because the Janjaweed would get them. The Janjaweed – like the bogeymen you tell your children about to stop them getting out of bed at night.
MARIAM	With her it did not stop at questions. Oh no. She would also come up with answers. "You will end up running this country one day," I told her. "Yes," she replied, "I'm going to be the first woman president of Sudan!"
IDRIS	But daddy was a man and they got him, so what's the point in hiding? And somebody's got to collect wood for the fire. How will we eat? I'm starving. "All right, all right," she said

	"Let's go and get some wood" See, I always knew how to get my own way with her.
MARIAM	When she was a little girl she'd play this game – run away from me, out of my sight. And I'd be frantic with fear, thinking that I had lost her or that she had been abducted.
IDRIS	The two men seemed to appear from nowhere. They balanced rifles across their shoulders and sat on huge great horses. They just stood there staring at us, literally looking down on us. They got off their horses never losing hold of the guns – it was like a synchronised dance they had rehearsed a million times. One of them pointed his rifle at me and said, "Come here." Mesmerised by the gun I did what he told me. He lifted my robe with his rifle and asked me what I had hidden under there. Mother ran at him screaming, her fist held high. But he caught hold of her hand and held it, teasing her – laughing like a playful lover.
MARIAM	Come back my daughter.
IDRIS	Musa Hilal, a Janjaweed leader, once denied that there was a campaign of rape against black African women. He said, "Why would we rape them? They disgust us. Black women have such wanton sexual habits, as can be seen from the way they dance, that there would be no need for anyone to use force with them." They forced my mother to watch as they took turns to rape me.
MARIAM	Then you would hear a giggle high above you and there she would be.
IDRIS	When they had had enough of being watched they beat my mother unconscious and took me back to their camp. I do not know how long I was held there. (*Pause.*) I think she suffered the greater violence: She watched as her

daughter was repeatedly raped and could do nothing about it.

(*The lights change back to original state.*)

MARIAM I can only guess what you must have been through and my heart bleeds for you, but I am afraid that you are not my daughter.

IDRIS Then this is worse than anything that has happened to me up until now.

MARIAM (*gently*) But you are right I do have a daughter.

IDRIS Yes, yes you do.

MARIAM But she is many miles from here. She is a fighter with the rebel army, you see. The JEM. Justice and Equality Movement. She's always been the kind of girl who couldn't sit back and just let things happen to her – she's the sort who has to take action. She carries a gun – a Kalashnikov – and she knows how to use it. She has been trained to make bombs. I suppose I shouldn't tell you these things because you can't trust anybody these days. As far as I know you might be a government spy, but I can't help being proud. Every time I hear a government installation has been blown up I think, "That's my girl!"

IDRIS (*crestfallen*) Yes, you must be very proud.

MARIAM So, now will you let me go?

(IDRIS *moves out of* MARIAM'S *path*.)

MARIAM It's too late to go looking for firewood now. I think I'll leave it until tomorrow. No doubt you will try to stop me again, won't you? It's very touching the way you young ones protect us oldies. Your mother would be proud of you, too. The way you haven't given up looking for her. Good luck with your search.

(MARIAM *goes*.)

IDRIS (*direct to audience*) You're asking yourselves which one of them is mad? Which story is true? One of them is deluded, but which one? Sometimes I too think that I must have dreamt all this – the bad men on horseback make for a romantic picture, don't you think? But no matter how hard I pinch myself this nightmare will not go away . . .

When the Janjaweed finally let me go I wandered around until I reached home again. It was that moment of silence I remember. That moment, just before reality ignites into motion. Not one bird singing, nothing stirring in the long grass, no flies buzzing even with all the dead just lying there like abandoned dolls. They had not even begun to smell yet. Just the sickly sweet scent of smoke from a fire that had recently gone out, leaving only ashes.

(*Lights fade.*)

GIVE, AGAIN?

GIVE, AGAIN?

by Lynn Nottage

GIVE AGAIN? was first performed at the Tricycle Theatre, London, on 24th October 2006, as part of *How Long is Never? Darfur – a response*. The play was directed by Indhu Rubasingham and the cast was as follows:

WIFE   Jenny Jules

HUSBAND   Karl Collins

Set designed by Polly Sullivan
Costumes designed by Sydney Florence
Lighting design by Darren Murray
Sound design by Paul Kizintas

GIVE, AGAIN?

A sleek modern dining room. A stylish WOMAN, *thirties, sits at a table set for breakfast, thumbing through an unusually large pile of envelopes.*

WOMAN   Darling, Darfur or the rainforest?

(She calls to her husband, off stage.)

WOMAN   Darling, did you hear me? Darfur or the rainforest?

(An equally stylish MAN, *thirties, enters carrying a thermal French press and an interior design magazine tucked under his arm. He places the coffee press on the table before settling into a chair across from her.)*

MAN   I'm sorry, what are you asking me?

WOMAN   Darfur or the rainforest?

MAN   Is this some sort of geography quiz?

WOMAN   No, silly. I have a mountain of fundraising letters from advocacy groups all asking for our help in some way or another.

(She thumbs through the letters.)

Darfur, Darfur. Darfur. Darfur . . . and one for the rainforest in the Congo.

(She looks up at him.)

WOMAN   New shirt?

MAN   You like?

WOMAN   It's a little snug.

(*The* MAN *sucks in his belly.*)

WOMAN Darling, do you want to give?

MAN Give, again?

WOMAN Yes. It's urgent, they're using words like 'dire' and 'desperate'.

MAN But didn't we give to Darfur around this time last year? Wasn't there something rather serious going on then?

WOMAN Yes, we did. But Darling, it appears it's still going on?

MAN (*shocked*) How is that possible? One year later. If I recall we made out a check for $100. Yes, it was $100.

WOMAN Actually, it was only seventy-five.

MAN (*indignant*) Well, seventy-five!

WOMAN Yes, but look at this pile! I'm thinking maybe we should have given more, you stopped me, remember, because you wanted the large and pricey thermal French press.

MAN So what? I did, and it turned out to be one of our better buys.

WOMAN That is true, a good cup of coffee is so important in the morning, but darling we really should have given them $100 last year. I feel awful.

MAN Oh, stop it. I won't be made to feel guilty about this thing, not during breakfast. That's what they want, that's how they get you, but it isn't our fault. We gave. And what have they, them, those people who mediate and take our donations been doing between now and then? Huh? It was crisis a year ago, for God's sake. So, why is it still going?

WOMAN	I don't know, that's a very fair question. I'm sure there's a reasonable answer. If you ask me, someone at the United Nations appears to be a very sound sleeper.
MAN	You're not kidding. Last year didn't they suggest rather strongly that we help stop it now or else . . . or else, it was all very was ominous. Or else!! (*Thinking.*) What is the trouble there again?
WOMAN	Genocide.
MAN	Genocide? My, that's a strong word. Are you sure? If true, it's unfortunate. But I find that word is being bandied about quite a bit these days, it's like the new human rights trend. "Genocide." An oldie but a goodie.
WOMAN	Oh, stop it. It's serious.
MAN	Then tell me this, how in God's name can it go on for over a year and our government still hasn't stepped in to stop it?
WOMAN	Why are you asking me all of the difficult questions this morning? I don't know.

(*A moment.*)

MAN	It's things like this that make you stop reading the newspaper. Coffee?
WOMAN	Yes, please.

(*He presses down the French press and pours the coffee.*)

WOMAN	And will you break me off half of the croissant?
MAN	Just take the whole thing.
WOMAN	I don't want the whole thing.

MAN	But you will want it in a moment, so why not just place the whole thing on your plate now. There, was that difficult?

WOMAN	I don't want the whole thing. Oh, Darling, leave it alone.

(*They sip their coffee in silence.*)

(*suddenly*) Do you think we should give again?

MAN	Give, again?

WOMAN	Yes, that's what I'm asking.

MAN	We gave last year and it didn't make one bit of difference, so no.

WOMAN	No? Did you say, no? Did I hear you correctly? No?

MAN	Why did you ask my opinion if you're going to be so surprised by my response. What can we do, keep giving and giving, while nothing and nothing keeps happening? I'd rather spend the money on new set of flatware.

WOMAN	(*incensed*) What are you saying?

MAN	What am I saying? I'm saying that I did something, which is far more than most the people we know.

WOMAN	Oh, maybe you're right. We did. I don't think any of our friends have done anything. So we're way ahead of the curve. I feel good about that. I do. But I still find it a little hard to hear about what's going on there. It is such a mess, and you know how I hate messy things. Listen to this letter . . .

(*The* WOMAN *opens the envelope. Out pours the sounds of the chaos of war. Gunfire, pounding hooves, screams of despair. Unbearable. A huge gust of wind blows dust and tumbleweeds across the stage.*)

MAN   They got all of that into the letter? Jesus Christ. It's chilling.

WOMAN   And that's one of the easier to stomach. I've only been through half the pile and I'm absolutely mortified . . . that we gave so little last year.

MAN   Are all of those like that?

WOMAN   Yes.

(*The* WOMAN *hands the man the envelopes. He opens one. The desperate wail of a child. A scream. He shuts it. He opens another. Angry shouting. Gunfire. He shuts it abruptly.*)

WOMAN   And you want another set of flatware?

MAN   Don't rub it in. I thought it would be nice to have . . . nevermind.

WOMAN   Darling don't laugh, but . . . but if we don't give this year, maybe we should participate in the demonstration that's happening next month.

MAN   Us?

WOMAN   Yes. Why not us?

MAN   Because we're not those kinds of people, we don't do those sorts of thing.

WOMAN   And why shouldn't we take a stand?

MAN   You mean like standing out in the cold and shouting at a building for two hours?

WOMAN   Oh, I see what you mean. But they say it could get worse in Darfur.

MAN   Worse? What is worse than genocide?

WOMAN   I don't know, perhaps knowing that it's happening and doing nothing.

   (*Blackout.*)